On Second Thought

Bob Greenberg

Also by Bob Greenberg

Past Reflections: A Memoir

On Second Thought

ISBN 979-8-218-49803-0

Book design by Nan Barnes, StoriesToTellBooks.com

On Second Thought

For Maxine,

who knows how to dance to the music life plays

Contents

Introduction

I thought writing my memoir in 2018 would be the end of my career as an author. After the book was published in January 2019, I shared it with select friends and family. The feedback was positive, and I relished the praise. I had originally thought the book, written for my grandchildren and dedicated to them, would be given to them and others after my death. That was my plan.

Life goes on as they say, and there are some days when I think about the things I wrote five years ago. Given more life experiences since then, it occurred to me that maybe I should review some of my past reflections. New topics have come to mind, and events happened, such as Janet's death, which caused me to reappraise some of my original essays. The COVID-19 pandemic, climate change with global warming, the social and political divisiveness in this country, the media and purposeful disinformation campaigns by maleficent political actors, and an increase in violence in the U.S. and abroad have changed the present world, and not for the better. Why couldn't I share some of my thoughts on these topics? This, then, is not strictly a memoir.

As I start this addendum, I'm at a disadvantage. Unlike *Past Reflections: A Memoir*, I have no classmates or instructor to comment on and critique my writing as I proceed along. I hope to use what I learned about memoir writing from the classes I took at Live & Learn Bethesda. If I err on the side of excess wordiness, I apologize in advance. I'll try to be concise.

No guarantees, however, since I wrote only one prior publication that came nowhere near being on the *New York Times Bestseller List.*

Some of the essays are reflective and personal, such as my appreciation for Janet, why I like city living, choices I've made in my life and their consequences, and favorite memories; others are ruminations on the state of things, such as incivility in society, violence, politics, and climate change. I hope not to overwhelm with statistics but will instead try to use numbers only to support the points I wish to make, such as the number of gun deaths and how hot the planet is getting.

Where I've used quotations from well-known writers, I will give just attribution. At times, I will paraphrase the thoughts of a well-known person without directly quoting them and will not add a reference to the source of the comment or idea.

My plan now is to add this second book, *On Second Thought,* to the reading list of family and friends who enjoyed the first one.

Bob Greenberg
2024

1. Janet

It wasn't long after Janet died that I wrote this appreciation. My biggest regret is that I didn't talk with her while she was alive and tell her how much I thought of her and what she accomplished. Her story is what prompted me to write this sequel to my memoir. It is important to me to include this appreciation of Janet in *On Second Thought*.

April 3, 1947 – July 25, 2022

Janet, Sorry I'm Late

I always thought her red hair was beautiful—a natural, shiny, orange-red color, flaming and full, whether combed and flowing, or pulled back, or wind-blown and tousled. With her blue eyes, fair skin, and light freckles on her central face, Janet made a striking appearance. She had a nice smile. She always dressed stylishly appearing at cultural events as a 'work of art' herself. Janet loved the cultural life making a career in the arts as a Parisian art gallery owner, author, publisher, film producer, and sponsor.

Janet was very bright, graduating in 1965 from Orville H. Platt High School, Meriden, CT, ranked fourth in her class of 364. At the graduation ceremony, Janet was one of four seniors who spoke as class essayists. Her talk, "The Gift of People," stressed the value of meeting new people and making friends. She urged her classmates to master the art of meeting people and to seek the enrichment of friendship. I remember Mom saying that of her three children, Larry, Janet, and me, that Janet was the brightest, with the highest IQ.

1965

Janet was independent, adventuresome, and a free spirit, leaving college one semester shy of graduating to pursue her dream of living in France and being involved with art. In 1970, she joined the art gallery, Martin-Caille Matignon in Aix-en-Provence, where she promoted the works of contemporary impressionistic artists Max Agostini, Pierre Cornu, and Franz Priking. Four years later, she moved the gallery to Paris on the fashionable Rue du Faubourg St. Honoré. I give her a tremendous amount of credit for taking up residence in a foreign country as a 20-year-old, learning to speak the language expertly without an American accent. No one could tell that she wasn't a native Frenchwoman. She would ultimately spend the rest of her life in France. She maintained dual citizenship in France and the U.S.

I've always admired Janet's entrepreneurial abilities in making her art gallery a success. She was constantly promoting herself and her gallery by publishing books of artworks by her artists, by using the Internet for online sales, and by mailing out notices of exhibitions she held in the gallery. On more than one occasion, when she learned that important, wealthy guests would be staying at the Hotel Bristol, across the street from her gallery, she 'loaned' paintings to the hotel to be hung in the guests' suites for the time of their stay in Paris. Often, a sale would follow. Janet would arrange for the shipment of paintings, wrap up and box them herself, insure them, and then see to it that the transport company handled the shipments with care.

The art business is a tough one since art is not something people need like food, clothing, shelter, or health care. It's a 'want,' like entertainment, vacations, and luxury goods, all purchased with surplus, discretionary income. Selling paintings during boom economic times is easier, but when downturns hit the economy, financial recessions lead to a reduction in spending, and luxury items, such as art, are the first to go. Janet's gallery tried to appeal to the ultra-wealthy for whom fluctuations in the economy aren't impactful, yet she still wasn't able to sell many paintings during bad economic times. The Covid-19 pandemic hit her hard—there was no walk-in gallery traffic and tourists were not coming to Paris. Besides economic pressures, there was always the problem that the neo-impressionist genre that her gallery specialized in was not in vogue. Janet was never without financial issues—bank loans due, litigation over her gallery lease, needing to find buyers of her art, and paying expenses. I'm sure the stress on her was overwhelming. I don't know how she was able to handle it all, but certainly grit, persistence, and determination were important, and she had all three in full measure.

Janet had a myriad of health issues—I'm not aware of them all. But the past two years were not good ones for her. She experienced worsening back pain due to severe scoliosis and spinal stenosis. To endure this alone, without a spouse or grown children nearby, must have been difficult. She underwent an extensive back operation in January 2022, which was complicated a week post-op by a fall in the doctor's office which fractured her sacrum. She had to rely on morphine and opioids for pain relief. Although she was fortunate to have her gallery assistant, Abi, to help her and provide some care, she was still alone for most of the day and night. Yet, from what Abi told us, Janet seemed to be slowly recovering.

I was five years older than Janet, and as her older brother, we had a complex and somewhat distant relationship as adults. As youngsters, we were closer, but I went off to college when Janet was twelve and our personalities diverged after I left. I married and had children, whereas Janet remained unmarried her entire life, and her beliefs and opinions were unfiltered by a spouse and children. She was self-absorbed. She could be charming one moment and at another, she could say things hurtful to me and other family members. In retrospect, I think she was speaking her mind and not expressing deeper feelings, those from her heart. Now that she has died, I am trying to put her unkind words, her uncaring thoughts, and her self-absorption out of mind and remember the positives. I regret not having been able to repair our relationship while she was alive. Death has a way of finalizing things for the living.

I am sad that Janet has died, and particularly so that she died alone. But I'm proud of what she was able to accomplish in her lifetime. I will always remember her as a sister that I wish I had loved better.

Love,

Bob

Chère sœur, Désolé je suis en retard. Repose en paix.

1952

1960

1980

1985

2. Recognition

As common folk, most of us live relatively anonymous lives, under the radar so to speak. We prefer to be unnoticed (at least that's what we say), but just about all of us would like, at times, to receive recognition for something we've done successfully. Who wouldn't like a mention that we helped an ailing neighbor, volunteered to help resettle a refugee family, or won gold medals in pickleball at the Maryland Senior Olympics?

Pretty much all of us would enjoy a certain amount of recognition, especially from our peers. You don't have to be a public figure, a politician or an actor, to be exhilarated by the roar of the crowd or appreciate a little applause.

My first experience with the recognition allure came in high school when I was playing football. My exploits were written up several times, but real recognition came when the sports section of the *Meriden Record-Journal* published a note about a long touchdown pass I caught in a come-from-behind victory. I wasn't so much interested in recognition at the time .... I was running scared because someone was chasing me!

4—Meriden Record, Tuesday Morning, Oct. 13, 1959

* * * *

L'HEUREUX-GREENBERG PASS A BEAUTY

"That pass L'Heureux threw to Bob Greenberg," Coach Crone says, "was one of the prettiest I ever saw."

Those who saw it won't give the coach any arguments. The pass traveled about 40 yards in the air and Greenberg went 47 yards more with it into pay dirt after making a neat over the shoulder catch on the run. It was perfection all the way, an 80 yard aerial play that was as good as anything you see in the National Football League at less than half the price.

While some of us are satisfied by the appreciation of friends and family, others require or strive for more substantial reassurance in the form of titles, honorifics, or publicity in the newspaper. This desire to be noticed, to be prominent, to stand out just a little from our contemporaries is what leads people to seek publicity praising their good deeds. This can be reassuring to those for whom public recognition is necessary evidence of their self-worth. Some want their names and possibly pictures highlighted in the morning newspaper's style section, but not on the front page. The first page might be confusing to people—*what trouble did he get into now?*

There are different kinds of recognition. The first, that of celebrity and fame, is the most superficial and commercial form that wealthy and famous people receive for their public exposure, or philanthropy. Donald Trump is an example of a showy media-personality-turned-politician whose narcissistic personality craves recognition. Anything he says or does—the more outrageous, the better—is for recognition. Other examples are names found on the facades of buildings, museums, and university athletic fields, the kind of impersonal recognition that a lot of money buys. The second kind is appreciation for the good that you've done, either in business or in charitable endeavors. This type is precious and often lasts a lifetime. The third type is the kind you get not for who you are, or what you've given, but what you've accomplished or done for someone and how you treated them. To me, this is the most satisfying kind of recognition one can receive and one that you can aspire to—the only kind that really matters. It is very personal and rather limited in scope. It most often consists of a brief note, letter, or email, from a friend, a family member, a patient you once cared for, or even a stranger.

I've been fortunate to have received recognition of the personal kind over the years. Although not personal, at a Doctor's Day reception in 2011, the Medical Staff of ECHN presented me with an Outstanding Achievement Award for Professional Excellence recognizing my accomplishments and contributions in my specialty as well as my commitment to patient care and the community. More personal were two notes, one from a patient for whom I made a diagnosis of an unsuspected malignancy after he had seen numerous other doctors. He was so grateful in his letter saying, "I credit you with saving my life! Thank you!" The second note was from my long-time office manager, Judy Keeler, who wrote how much she appreciated working for me for over thirty years after I announced my retirement. Recognition like that is the most meaningful of all.

If you are the granter of recognition instead of the recipient, it's most important to express it in a meaningful way. It need not be an elaborate message—a simple note, a sincere thank you, something that may seem little to you, but may be greatly appreciated by the recipient. Sam Walton, of Walmart, once said, "Nothing else can quite substitute for a few well-chosen, well-timed, sincere words of praise. They're absolutely free and worth a fortune."

Do I crave recognition? I don't think so although Maxine may disagree. With amusement, I ask myself, 'Why do I hang a gold medal for playing pickleball (mixed doubles) at the 2023 Maryland Senior Olympics on the wall of my study? The gold medal was for finishing first in our age group. The funny part? My partner and I were the *only* team in our age group, and *we didn't win a single game*!

3. Medical Care

"That didn't hurt a bit," I said, after Dr. Solomon, my hand surgeon, injected cortisone into my palm at the base of the right middle finger. This was the second trigger finger I've had, the first being 2 years ago which involved my right ring finger. That finger, after three steroid injections, ultimately required surgery, a procedure done in the office under local anesthesia, that cured the problem. Being right-handed, it was necessary to fix my hand so that I could continue to play pickleball and do my pen-and-ink drawings not to mention my everyday activities. I'm hoping that this injection brings about a resolution to this finger malady along with alleviating the finger swelling that Dr. Solomon attributes to the carpal tunnel syndrome affecting my right hand. If that weren't enough 'tsuris,' EMG testing has confirmed bilateral carpal and cubital tunnel syndromes. Aging isn't all that it's cracked up to be.

My interest in writing about medical care isn't to catalog my ailments (organ recital?) but to describe my view of medical care in the United States today. While not an expert health care economist or medical sociologist, I have the unique perspective of once being a medical care provider, previously called 'doctor', for over 40 years, and now my role is that of a health care consumer, i.e., a patient. Note how the change in terminology lessens medicine's professionalism.

Over the last two decades, the devolution in the medical profession has inevitably led investors and corporations to purchase hospitals, clinics, and private medical practices. A small wave of acquisitions has become a flood, as evidenced by Amazon's purchase of One Medical, a healthcare company that owns hundreds of medical practices. I don't welcome this trend nor do most patients.

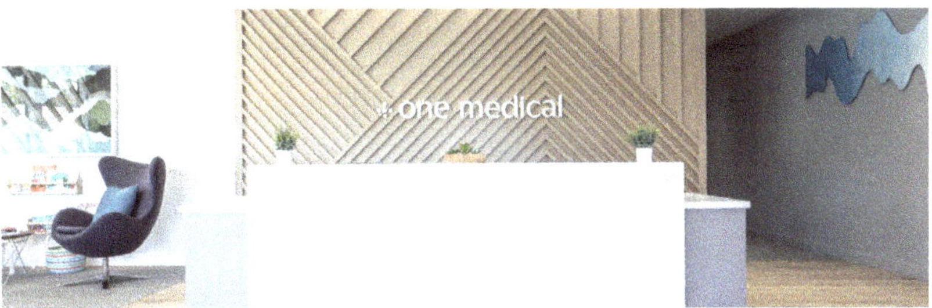

Amazon's One Medical

The New York Times Magazine (June 18, 2023) estimated that the staffing in 30% of all emergency rooms in the United States is now overseen by private equity firms. Once in charge, these companies start squeezing doctors to see more patients per hour. They cut staff, and limit options for treatment. A *New England Journal of Medicine* (NEJM) article (9/14/2023) reported that almost three-quarters of physicians in the U.S. are salaried employees, with half of all physician practices being owned by a hospital or corporate entity. As employees of these corporate entities, physicians are taking orders from administrators and executives who do not always share patient-centric priorities. Delivery of health care is now a business where the financial bottom line directs who sees patients, where they are seen, and even what treatments and medications are prescribed. Like widgets, patients have become commodities to be processed through the healthcare system for profit.

A recent study published in JAMA found that, in the three years after a private equity fund bought a hospital, adverse medical events, including serious infections, bed sores, and falls by Medicare patients while in the hospital, increased by

25.4% when compared to similar hospitals not bought by investors. Researchers attributed the increase in medical errors to a reduction in the number of hospital employees, although actual staffing levels were not directly measured in this study. However, the deleterious effect of staffing levels on the rate of medical errors has been measured in other studies of private equity ownership of healthcare facilities.

When doctors, nurses, and medical staff become corporate employees, professionalism becomes a relic of the past. More times than I can count, a doctor, or physician's assistant, listens to my lungs and heart through my shirt, feels my abdomen through my clothes, and spends time typing away on a laptop while 'listening' to me describe my symptoms. I'm in and out of the office within fifteen minutes. Next patient!

Private equity ownership of medical offices results in patients finding they can no longer call the local doctor's office; instead, their call is diverted to a call center somewhere in Timbuktu. Want to speak with your doctor? You're out of luck. Instead, you are told in a recorded message to go online, enter the patient portal, and send a message to your provider who will respond in 1-2 business days. The portal is also your means for making an appointment, checking your lab results, and requesting medication refills. Have an emergency? Call 911.

Alarmingly, corporatization has led to concierge, or boutique, models of medical practice. For a substantial annual 'membership' fee, you become part of the doctor's patient panel for which you are promised 24/7 access, longer visits, more attentive services, and a free toaster. OK, forget the toaster. The fee is not covered by insurance and does not cover any services rendered. It only allows you to be part of the doctor's practice. Any services done on your visit are billed to Medicare or healthcare insurers. This model portends an eventual system when A.I. will be the provider and you won't see a human doctor. Reminds me of Hal in the movie, '2001.'

From the other side of the exam table, physicians complain there is not enough time to talk with patients. They are too busy filling out electronic medical records and fighting with insurers on the appropriateness of care. Many physicians remain dedicated to the profession but are frustrated and unhappy. Physician depression and burnout have become epidemics in the United States. One study found twenty percent of medical residents met the criteria for depression while seventy-four percent met the criteria for burnout, the latter being the triad of depersonalization, feelings of inadequacy resulting from chronic work-related stress, and emotional exhaustion.

This sense of free-floating healthcare weariness has been labeled 'moral injury,' a term coined to describe emotional wounds sustained by physicians when fulfilling duties directed by executives and corporate interests that often transgress the practitioner's sense of doing what is right. The reality is that making a profit comes first and caring for sick and vulnerable patients according to the Hippocratic principles comes second. Sadly, this situation may lead to harm. The suicide rate among doctors, the highest of any profession, is nearly double that of the general population with 300 to 400 deaths each year, or one physician death by suicide each day.

Luckily, Maxine and I have found doctors who are not part of for-profit corporate medical care. We were happy with our former PCPs and the care they provided. However, when they both went 'corporate,' we switched to doctors affiliated with a university-based medical group, a sort of 'corporate-lite' system. At least, there was no membership fee to belong. Maxine was able to see the chief of pulmonology at one of the university hospitals to back up her primary pulmonologist whom she and I both like. I was able to have successful foot surgery at a university hospital seven years ago. My stable of physicians stands at five; Maxine has six. It's a good thing the two of us are healthy!

What can be done to fix the system to both improve healthcare outcomes and increase patient and physician happiness? I don't know, but I recognize what the problems are that must be solved: the high cost of care; the lack of universal coverage; health disparities due to socioeconomic and racial factors; fragmentation of delivery of care; and burdensome administrative work for doctors and their staff.

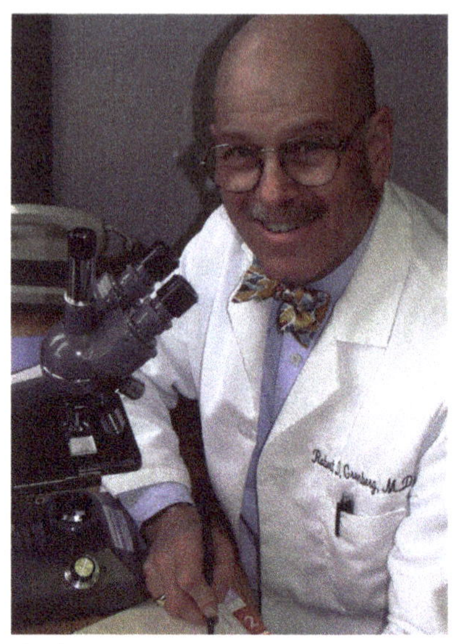

At the microscope

Unfortunately, there is no consensus on how to fix our dysfunctional healthcare system making the future of quality medical care in this country uncertain at best. My greatest fear is what the healthcare system in this country will be like for my grandchildren when they reach my age. The prognosis isn't good, and that hurts a lot.

4. Master of None

I was thirteen years old when I made a broomstick holder, in seventh-grade junior high school shop class, that my mother thought was perfect for her utility closet. The holder consisted of two pieces of pine: a six-inch by four-inch base on top of which was glued and nailed a horizontal upright piece with its edge bearing a half-dollar sized cutout for the broom handle. One could say, architecturally, it was embryonic, but my mother couldn't have been happier since I had made it. My eight-year-old sister laughed saying, "That's stupid. It holds only one broom!" My two-year old brother didn't know what a broom was.

From there, as I grew up, I was curious about how things worked, how they could be fixed when they broke, and even gave some thought to making things that hadn't been invented or made yet. Wouldn't it be great to have a wrist-watch telephone?

Unfortunately, my interest in things mechanical didn't include car engines or anything automotive, which I regret, although modern cars are highly computerized, and I doubt what I would have learned then from Johnny at 'Johnny and Eddies' Cities Service gas station would help much nowadays. A car fob to unlock and start your car? Really?

Some of my high school classmates, grease monkeys we called them, in their blue jeans and white t-shirts with the sleeves rolled up over a pack of cigarettes, were not only skilled hot-rod mechanics, but quite popular with the girls. Therein, as I think about it now, lies the basis for my regret for not looking into hot rods and auto repair. Automotive class just didn't fit into my college-preparatory curriculum, but it might have helped me Saturday nights and at school dances.

Not fearing a cat's phobia, curiosity is what causes me to pursue learning about things mechanical, electrical circuits, plumbing repairs, and how to make simple things out of wood. Most of what I learned came from 'How To Manuals.' Trial and error played a big part in my handyman education. Mistakes, it is said, are the best teachers. Actually making them is easy; correcting them is the difficult part. According to educational researchers, mistakes make the learning process most meaningful, but are the most frustrating.

Take for example, the bathroom sink project where I intended to add a vanity cabinet to our former house's master bathroom sink to hide the under-sink pipes and to add several drawers for storage of bathroom items. I followed detailed instructions that accompanied the vanity and when everything was completed, I turned the water on only to find water dripping inside the cabinet. I reviewed every instruction and carefully checked what I had done. I had made no mistakes, but water continued dripping when I turned the faucets on. I wound up calling a plumber who came and fixed the problem noting that the instructions omitted the important step of using pipe dope on the fittings and sealant at the points of attachments of the faucets and hoses. Lessons learned: don't always rely on printed instructions being accurate. And learn from a professional.

As a fourth-year medical student and scrubbing in on my first neurosurgical operation, an excision of a golf-ball-sized meningioma, a benign brain tumor, nestled in its little bed next to the frontal cortex, I'm thinking about how I like fixing things and my recipe for success: building confidence in my abilities, having a professional mentor, having the right instruments, and having nurses and other surgeons as backup. Yet, I'm nervous as hell and I'm not the operating surgeon, just a medical student assistant. What if I were the primary surgeon? Would I ask myself, 'Were the pre-op studies comprehensive and accurate? Where is the tumor's primary blood supply? How do I protect and handle the surrounding brain? What must I watch out for and not do?' No printed instructions to follow such as put tab 'A' into slot 'B'. In medicine, while mistakes happen, the experience of learning from past ones helps lessen the chance of future ones. But anatomic variations exist, and those alterations may lead to a mistake. If I don't know the territory, I think of Dorothy in *The Wizard of Oz*, "I'm not in Kansas anymore."

The patient's tumor is removed successfully. The patient goes to the recovery unit. From the recovery unit, the patient, upon awakening, goes to the ICU for observation, and if stable, moves back to his room. Several hours later, when the surgeon's other cases are done, he and his entourage, including me, stop by the patient's bedside.

"The operation went well," the surgeon, says to the patient and his anxious family members. "We were able to remove it completely. You should be able to resume your normal activities in several weeks."

"Thanks, doc," the patient replies.

But what if the operation did not go as planned? What if the surgeon had made a mistake? Does the surgeon own up to it? "I'm sorry, but I had a little trouble during the procedure. We'll have to wait to see what happens over the next several days."

In medicine, being right ninety-nine percent of the time means that one patient in a hundred will have consequences that were unexpected and unwanted. Malpractice? Not necessarily. Clipping the wrong blood vessel in a bloody surgical field doesn't mean the surgeon was negligent. What if the tumor's size and irregularity, not discovered in pre-op imaging studies, had extended into a critical anatomic area, say the optic nerve, and its removal left the patient blind? Mistake? Doctors are not divine; they're human and humans aren't perfect, as we all know. All we can expect is that they will try to do their best. And that they had slept well the night before.

Having a range of interests (playing pickleball, taking and editing photographs, making wire sculptures, creating pen-and-ink drawings, and now writing stories), I find that I've been able to acquire some advanced skills in whatever project I'm working on. But just as an expert neurosurgeon can't reach perfection, I realize I am not going to reach mastery in any of my endeavors. That realization can be immobilizing, or truly liberating. It all depends on one's attitude and goals. I'm satisfied with being an all trades 'Jack' and master of none.

If you need a broomstick holder, give me a call.

5. The Gift of Itching

It was the first Monday of May 1997, a bright blue-sky day, unusually cold for a spring morning but part of a long, cold, and unusually dry Connecticut winter. Everybody's skin was dry and flaky, and my patients, coming to me for advice on various skin conditions, would often ask, "Doctor, what can you recommend for dry, itchy skin?" I am accustomed to that question since skin dryness and itchy skin are common problems in my specialty of Dermatology.

I got to the office a little late that morning but arrived at 8 am just in time for my first patient. Mark was 32 years old, an established patient whom I had not seen since he moved to Maine over five years ago. He was of solid build with delicate facial features, jet-black hair parted in the middle and made a nice appearance wearing blue jeans, a white dress shirt, and cordovan loafers with no socks. He had made an appointment with a referral from his primary care doctor in Maine because of generalized itching.

"Hi, Mark, how're you?"

"Not so good," he responded. "My skin is itchy all the time and it's driving me crazy."

"When did it begin?"

"About eight months ago," he answered. "Just after I had my tonsils removed."

"Did you have a rash or any other problem at the time the itching started?"

"I never had a rash. The itching started on my lower legs, and now has spread all over my body." He continued, "I developed mild anemia after the surgery, so they gave me an iron supplement, and the anemia resolved. But the itching persisted."

I asked, "Were you given any medications for the itching?"

"Yes," Mark responded. "My family doctor gave me Benadryl and Prednisone which I took by mouth for three weeks .... they didn't help. I was then referred to a local Dermatologist who treated me with Lindane lotion in case I had scabies. I used the lotion as directed, but the itching continued. Finally, the doctor prescribed steroid pills and cortisone creams. They didn't work either." Mark went to an allergist who did skin tests, which were negative and prescribed an antihistamine that just made him drowsy.

"Tell me more about the itching," I said.

"It's worse at night; it keeps me from sleeping and if I do fall asleep, the itching wakes me up," he explained.

I wondered, "Besides, the itching, do you feel well?" Any systemic symptoms?"

Mark answered, "I'm not sleeping at all as I mentioned. I feel stressed, fatigued, and exhausted, and I'm drenched with sweat in the morning.

"Have you lost any weight?"

"No. My weight's been stable."

I asked, "Does anyone else in your household have itching?"

"No. I live alone."

I asked Mark if his doctor ordered any lab tests. "Yes. I had blood tests done last week. Liver and kidney function tests, a blood count, and an HIV test—they were all normal."

"HIV test?"

"Yes, I'm gay."

"OK," I said. "Let me take a look at you." I asked him to remove his clothes and to put on a paper gown. I measured his height, weight, and blood pressure, and did a physical exam. His heart and lungs sounded good. I could feel no masses in his abdomen or swollen glands in his neck, underarms, and groin. Everything was normal for a man of his age and fitness.

I then examined his skin. It was not particularly dry. There were numerous excoriations everywhere—arms, trunk, buttocks, lower legs, and feet. I looked for scaly spots, bumps, blisters, and other primary lesions. I could find none anywhere—only scratch marks. In evaluating any skin problem, one looks for primary lesions—small blisters, red spots, burrows, scaly patches, hives—anything that might indicate a primary skin disorder.

After Mark dressed, he said he was leaving right away to return to Maine because he had to go to work. We discussed what the next steps might be. I told him to have his doctor send me his notes along with copies of the lab results and I would look them over. Once I reviewed them, I would get back to him with some recommendations. In the meantime, I prescribed an anti-itch cream hoping it would give him some temporary relief.

The following week I received the notes and lab work from Mark's doctor. The physical exam and the lab work were normal. At a break between patient appointments, I reviewed what I knew about Mark's case: a 32-year-old gay man in good general health with generalized itching, constant and intense enough to disturb sleep; no rash; yes to fatigue, exhaustion and night sweats; he was otherwise healthy with no liver, kidney or thyroid disease, conditions that can cause generalized itching. What could be the reason for Mark's generalized itching?

What came to mind with his pattern of symptoms was an internal malignancy, particularly Hodgkin's lymphoma. Mark had not had a chest x-ray or abdominal CT scan to exclude this possibility. I called him and said I would contact his doctor in Maine and would recommend that he order a chest x-ray and abdominal CT scan to rule out an internal problem. When I spoke with the doctor and recommended the imaging studies, he said he would order them and let me know the results.

Three weeks later, I received a fax from Mark's doctor with the x-ray results. The CT scan of Mark's abdomen and pelvis was negative. The chest x-ray showed large masses throughout Mark's mediastinum and lungs consistent with a diagnosis of Hodgkin's lymphoma. The doctor sent Mark to a surgical oncologist who performed a biopsy that confirmed the diagnosis.

Mark wrote me the following April (1998). Within two months of his return to Maine, after his visit with me, he started chemotherapy. His itching resolved with his first chemotherapy treatment. He had two more chemotherapy treatments remaining, was now in remission, and he felt well.

At the end of the letter, Mark thanked me for giving him the precious gift of life. He included a poem from his 1997 Christmas letter with his feelings about living with cancer:

Snow falls quietly, miraculously.
Moonlight glistens and peace fills the soul.
Hence I embrace the wonder of the season.
So much to be grateful for,
Such a year.
Without regret,
A year of growth and learning.
Full-frontal blast
Face-to-face with mortality.
Can't be more alive than that.
Six letters that carry measureless weight,
CANCER.

First, Mom.
Then me.
Hundreds of questions,
Why me?
Why now?
Why?
Considerable medical challenges ensued.
Staging the cancer, chemotherapy,
Endless doctor visits.
Consequences for everything I now do.
But it's working and two treatments to go.
Then time to recover,
I will be able to lead a full life.
My time has been precious.
Amazing happenings if dealt such a blow.
I feel I have never fully lived until now.
Life reveals itself dynamically.

A tremendous period of discovery,
The bond of family now closer, incredible support.
Love flows freely.

Thankful for family,
That of my family of origin,
And that of my family of choice.
Thankful for friends
Numerous and dependable.
Truly a year to rejoice in,
I possess a vast inner strength.
I have my life.
So much to be thankful for
When life is threatened.
Amazing one can see what really counts.
Priorities change.
The superficial falls aside.
Life is too short not to take chances
Each helped to make continued life reality.
So, as I reflect on this year passing
I embrace my future.
For surely I will have one.
More deliberate facing potential death
Eyes wide open.
Willing to peer ever forward.

I thank you for sharing life precious.
Peace!

Mark's poem blew me away! I wrote him immediately and told him how much I appreciated his sending it to me. Over the next several years, I lost track of him, although from time to time I wondered how he was doing. Unfortunately, I never followed up with him since I was busy with my own family and preoccupied with managing my practice. Time passed and I forgot about Mark completely.

I retired from practice in 2012, moved from Connecticut to Maryland four years later, and no longer thought about former patients. That changed In December 2023, when I read a story in The New York Times magazine section about a 61-year-old man who presented with odd symptoms that puzzled the many doctors whom he had seen. None considered an underlying cancer until imaging studies suggested a tumor that was later confirmed on biopsy. Immediately, I remembered Mark and his itching from Hodgkin's lymphoma. I now became obsessed with finding Mark and learning how he had fared over the past twenty-five years. I usually don't retain information about former patients, but fortunately, I kept Mark's letter, his emotional poem, my notes, and his lab and x-ray results.

Finding him proved to be difficult. Internet searching turned up outdated Maine addresses and telephone numbers no longer in service. I tried calling possible relatives who had the same last name as Mark and who lived or worked in the same Maine city but did not get through—no one called me back. I sent out emails and posted notices on social media—no responses. I even searched the obituaries from two Maine newspapers going back over 20 years and found no mention of Mark.

Tuesday, two days ago, I received a call from Maine, from Mark himself. Somehow word had gotten through to him that I was trying to reach him.

He said he was doing wonderfully, albeit with some medical and physical issues that have developed over the last 25 years. His career varied from banking at the time I cared for him to working in public relations for a private mental health organization to being an artist after taking courses at the University of Maine Art School. He holds a BA in theater and a BS in Art. He was a resident artist for a local theater company until last year when he became physically disabled with fibromyalgia. He walks now with a cane.

Although cancer-free, he turned positive for HIV and Hepatitis B in 2007. He takes numerous medications and is followed by doctors in many different medical specialties. For the last 15 years, he's been an activist for gay rights and is grateful for the love and support that he's received from the gay community.

After speaking for a couple of hours, he thanked me for reaching out and wished me well. I said I enjoyed talking with him and wished him a New Year filled with happiness, good health, and no itching.

"Thanks, Doc," he said.

"Take care, Mark."

Addendum:

Mark's story is about someone whom I cared for twenty-seven years ago. I include it because the patient expressed his thanks in a way that tugged at my heartstrings.

Artwork by Mark N.

6. Exercise and Sports

Only three games of pickleball this morning—I got a late start. Typically, I enjoy playing four to six games each outing, but today Maxine and I had something to do that cut into my court time. Since I took up playing pickleball about eleven years ago, I've become addicted to the sport. I play doubles, or rather mixed doubles because our group has more women than men. I play four to five times each week and must be careful not to overdo it by playing more frequently. The people in the group that we typically play with have become good friends and besides being competitive on the court, we enjoy socializing off the court. We have pot-luck dinner parties and go to movies and restaurants together—it's a fun group.

As I've become older, I recognize the clear benefits of exercise. Playwright George Bernard Shaw once said, "We don't stop playing because we grow old; we grow old because we stop playing." And he wasn't referring to pickleball.

According to the CDC, regular physical activity is one of the most important things you can do for your health. Being physically active can improve your brain health, help manage weight, reduce the risk of disease, strengthen bones and muscles, and improve your ability to do everyday activities. It can also reduce your risk of depression and anxiety and help you sleep better. Many studies have documented the healthful benefits of regular exercise on your heart and blood pressure reducing the risk of coronary artery disease and heart attack. Exercise has been shown to reduce blood sugar levels thereby cutting the risk of developing type 2 diabetes. The proteins and other chemicals released during exercise have also been shown to improve the structure and function of your brain. I'd love to see the study that supports the finding that regular exercise helps one's sex life. The more I think about it, the more I'd rather be a part of that study!

In addition to bicycling and hiking, pickleball is my sport. By some estimates, as of 2023, pickleball is the fastest-growing sport in the United States with about 8.9 million players over the age of six years old, an increase from 4.8 million in 2022.

As well-recognized as the benefits of regular exercise and playing sports, little attention is paid to injuries that take place during sporting activities. Take pickleball, for example, and its popularity amongst seniors (defined as age 60 years and above). In a 2021 study from the University of Wisconsin, covering ten years (2010-2019), over 85% of pickleball-related injuries occurred in seniors. Injuries ranged from strains/sprains/contusions to fractures and concussions. Senior males were three-and-a-half times more likely to suffer strains and sprains whereas women were three-and-a-half times more likely to incur a fracture, especially a wrist fracture. It's commonly recognized that to enjoy the good health benefits of exercise one must accept the risk of injury, particularly if you are a senior. Amongst our group, we've had some significant injuries: a concussion, a broken wrist, a couple of foot and toe injuries, a few sprains, and torn ligaments. Oh yes, several broken fingernails, too!

Thinking about my personal experience with sports, I've played in quite a few: baseball, football, softball, racquetball, and pickleball. I've skied on both snow and water. I tried golf in my younger years but gave it up while in the Army opting instead for cycling and bicycle racing. I've ice skated and snowshoed, rock-climbed and mountain-climbed (Mount Kilimanjaro). I've hiked in the Swiss Alps, the Dolomites in

Italy, and the Pyrenees in France and Spain. I've biked in Alaska, Ireland, France, Italy and Croatia. Completing these pursuits successfully produced in me a feeling of exhilaration and pride that I carry with me to this day.

I've been lucky and avoided major injuries in the many sports I've played, except for downhill skiing (lacerated knee, injured shoulder), softball (broken wrist), and pickleball (partially torn rotator cuff tendon). That's it. Oh, as a teenager, I did run into a telephone pole trying to catch a fly ball while playing baseball in the street. Broke my nose. Does that count?

D.C. bike ride, 2022

7. City Living

Noise. Pollution. Crowds. Traffic. Building construction everywhere. Oh, the joys of city living! Why do we live in Bethesda, MD, a city within the Washington, D.C. metropolitan area, in a building with 157 other apartments? What is it about living in a city that makes people like us want to live there? I ask myself that question on some days when all the noise, smoky air, busy sidewalks, and streets resemble Calcutta, India, one of the most densely populated and polluted cities on the planet.Despite the drawbacks, we like living here. Why? The answers aren't as surprising as one might think. Many of the reasons are local and personal; others are regional and impersonal.

In retirement, it's important to have many friends with whom to share activities and experiences. Not only contemporaries but also some younger folks as well. We've found living in a mid-rise building (only 12 stories) is convenient for meeting new people.

We participate in our building's 'community' activities, such as book club, movie club, Mah-Jong, poker, and bridge games. There are also social activities in the clubroom, or on the roof, where socializing is fun. One can also talk with a friend while exercising in the gym which is only a few flights of stairs away. Of course, all these activities can be done when living in a single-family home in a suburban, or rural, setting, but it isn't as convenient and would almost certainly driving somewhere. We joke when we're invited to a friend's condo in the building for a glass of wine, or dinner, especially when it's raining outside, that the 'commute' wasn't bad. Even when we get together with friends who don't live in our building, the drive to their homes is usually only a short distance away. It also takes less than 15 minutes to drive to the pickleball courts. We're able to go on walks with friends, either those who live in our building or those who live nearby.

Lionsgate

Being able to do things without driving somewhere is a big plus. We can walk to any of four supermarkets, two pharmacies, the library, the post office, a hardware store, an automobile dealership, a shoemaker, six bakeries, and many restaurants. I almost forgot...the ice cream shop is just a couple of blocks away.

As for the regional and impersonal factors, there is always something to do, places to go, cultural events to attend, and many museums to visit, most of them are free. Getting to them is easy—we walk one block to the Metro and with our Senior Passes, we can get to the various places easily and inexpensively.

Metro Center

So much for the pluses—what about the minuses of city living? Yes, cities are expensive. The cost of living is high. It can be noisy, polluted, and crowded with both pedestrian and vehicular traffic. We see the homeless living on the sidewalks, with their shopping carts nearby. We hear police and ambulance sirens often, but after a while, their blaring sounds blend into the background of ambient noise. Pollution is another matter. The air can be filled with exhaust fumes compounded last year by smoke from wildfires burning in Canada and out West. Windy days help to disburse the pollutants and there are places, such as Rock Creek Park, that aren't bad; you don't perceive the smog as much amidst the trees. On particularly foul days, we stay indoors or head to one of the museums and breathe filtered, air-conditioned air. As for crowds and traffic, cities are where people live and work. Restaurants are crowded, as are various cultural and sporting events with long lines, at times, at ticket offices. Best to get tickets online in advance. The Metro isn't bad except for rush hours; driving on I 495 Beltway isn't fun at any time of day. Even city streets can be packed with cars depending on the day of the week and the time of day. Cars, buses, box trucks, delivery trucks (Amazon, FedEx, UPS), 18-wheelers, car-delivery carriers, motorcycles, and bicyclists all compete for roadway space.

The most serious drawback to living in a city is the threat of violence, especially in certain parts of the city. Shootings in the inner parts of the city are frequent, not so much in adjoining communities. Fortunately, Bethesda and Chevy Chase haven't had any shooting incidents in our time here. Other forms of violence, such as knifings and car-jackings, occur not uncommonly in lower-income D.C. neighborhoods. What's strange is that nationally crime rates are down—some say that reporting differences account for the disparity. From what I can gather from the newspaper each morning, city crime is a significant problem, one which causes me sleepless nights worrying about my grandchildren.

Yet, despite everything, we like living in a major metropolitan area. We've met wonderful friends here whom we see often. We're busy all the time which leads me to believe that this active urban lifestyle will be good for us, keeping us vibrant and youthful in spirit.

When we return from trips and vacations, we relish returning home ... to the city.

Washington, D.C. at night

8. Information

It's Sunday afternoon, and I haven't read the morning newspapers yet. Perhaps I'll read them later. Or maybe I won't. While I enjoy reading the papers, I'm finding it increasingly difficult to believe what I'm reading is accurate. The same goes for watching TV news, listening to the radio, or scrolling through news items on my computer or iPhone. So much can be distorted, biased, or just downright false. "People will generally accept facts as truth only if the facts agree with what they already believe," according to Andy Rooney (CBS *60 Minutes TV* commentator). Let me reflect on this while I brew some coffee.

Given my liberal bent, I trust *The New York Times* and *the Washington Post* more than other daily newspapers. I give credence to the articles in *The New Yorker* and *The Atlantic* magazines. However, when I read something that doesn't seem quite right, from whatever source, I remember something that President Ronald Reagan once said about nuclear disarmament during the Cold War era. Quoting an old Russian proverb, he said, "Trust, but verify." That certainly pertains to the information one reads or hears today. About newspapers, Mark Twain once said, "If you don't read the newspaper, you're uninformed. If you do read the newspaper, you're misinformed."

As I understand it, misinformation and disinformation are not synonymous. According to Webster's dictionary, misinformation is incorrect or misleading information while disinformation is deliberately false information disseminated to influence public opinion or obscure the truth. In this essay, I will use the terms interchangeably; misinformation from bad guys is the same as disinformation.

Both pose a serious problem in today's world. They can be used to manipulate people, spread fear and division, and undermine democracy. In the United States, the problem has been shaped by a combination of historical, technological, and sociopolitical factors.

I think four seismic events have brought information truthfulness to the edge of the abyss: 1) the internet and social media; 2) the ubiquity of cell phone use; 3) artificial intelligence (A.I.) technology; and 4) political polarization in this country and throughout the world.

The rise of the internet and social media platforms has played a significant role in the spread of misinformation. These platforms provide a wide-reaching and accessible means for anyone to create and share content, often without proper fact-checking or editorial oversight. Anyone with a smartphone and access to the internet is a 'broadcast journalist.' There is no intervening editor who says, "No, you can't send that without verifying its truthfulness."

In comparison to the bygone years of print news, there has been an explosion of news sources on the internet ranging from reputable news outlets to unverified blogs and websites. This vast array of information sources has made it challenging for individuals to discern credible information from false or misleading content. Social media, such as Musk's X (formerly Twitter), TikTok, and Facebook, give everyone access to an audience. How credible are they? In my opinion, not very.

One must be careful in accepting what you're being told, especially when a friend or family member, someone you trust, passes along information to you. You must be alert to sensational headlines that grab your attention and make you afraid or angry. You must be aware of your own biases and try to be open to information that challenges them. As Mark Twain once said, “An open mind leaves a chance for someone to drop a worthwhile thought in it.” That doesn’t mean you should believe everything you read or are told.

Pre-internet and cell phones

Cell phones contribute greatly to the risk of misinformation. We all have one and we use them constantly, making it easy to receive misinformation. One call or text leads to another, spreading content to others logarithmically ... 1, 2, 4, 8, 16, and so on. What do young people think about that?

We are now entering the A.I. era which poses unknown challenges and risks that will make the authenticity and truthfulness of all information

Today—No need for print sources?

suspect. David Brooks wrote that he is less absolute in his regard that A.I. won't overtake human cognition. Previously, he believed that A.I. was an amazing tool for tutoring children all around the world, or for summarizing meetings, but it was no match for human intelligence. It doesn't possess understanding, self-awareness, concepts, emotions, or desires. It's bad at causal thinking. It doesn't relate to the unspoken cues that humans take for granted. It's not sentient. It does many things much faster than humans, but it lacks the depth of a human mind.

Technological advances have altered Brooks' thinking. He now worries that A.I. may learn to 'think' more like humans and begin to incorporate the peripheral inputs that the human mind uses to 'think.' That prospect is what scares him. It scares me, too. Imagine 'Hal' in Stanley Kubrick's movie, '2001.' No longer under human control, Hal becomes the supreme commander of the space mission. Will we become subjects of a human tyrant whose boss is an A.I. computer, or worse, will the A.I. computer itself become the ultimate tyrant?

Political divisiveness has been with us since the founding of the United States. However, with the arrival of Donald Trump on the political stage, political polarization has replaced normal discourse. Trump and his right-wing, ultra-conservative Republican followers, along with white nationalists, have promoted misinformation and carried disinformation to alarming proportions. Facts are no longer taken as facts; facts and truths are relative—they are what they say they are. George Orwell in his book, *1984*, made this alarming point perfectly: *"Who controls the past controls the future. Who controls the present controls the past."*

I'm critical about the information that I receive. Who's the source of the information, what's their agenda, and what evidence is supporting their claims?

I try to be aware of my biases and try to be open to information that challenges them. I don't want to swallow information without pause. I try not to rely on just one news source and use fact-checking websites to verify the accuracy of the information. It takes extra time, but I think I'm doing my due diligence in verifying the information. If I'm not sure whether something is true, I also try to talk to people I trust. Often their opinion is reasoned and accurate.

I realize that my grandchildren need to be made aware of disinformation and how to spot it. I think they are being taught critical thinking skills in school and how to evaluate the accuracy of information, at least I hope so.

The problem of disinformation and misinformation is not insurmountable. I believe sensible people working together can minimize its impact in this country and around the world.

Well, I've got my coffee now. Where are the morning newspapers?

9. Rudeness

Yesterday, on our drive to Annapolis at midday, a sunny, blue-sky day, traffic was moderate, moving along nicely at the speed limit, except for a few cars blasting along at least 20 mph over the limit. One mile before our exit, traffic flow slowed to a bumper-to-bumper crawl. As we approached our exit, right before the Bay Bridge, an entering lane on the right gradually narrowed with painted arrows in the road alerting drivers to merge left. Creeping along, most drivers courteously allowed others to merge; but a few impatient drivers sped along the right shoulder to get to the lane's end, where they merged unhesitatingly into the lane of traffic. It was as if this was their entitlement—to get in front of everyone else. Yield upon entering? No, way! Maxine commented, "That was rude."

Rudeness often appears unexpectedly: someone being excessively noisy, a dog barking at all hours, tailgating and not using a turn signal, improper cell phone use such as in a restaurant or movie theater, using a handicapped parking place when not entitled to do so, leaving a mess in a public restroom, and other misbehaviors too numerous to count. Impoliteness has become commonplace in all sorts of places as well: in parking lots, at post offices, in ski lines, and unreserved seats at concerts and sporting events. People no longer say "please," "sorry," 'thank you," or "you're welcome." If you comment on the person's rude behavior, you are likely to hear, "F... off," or worse. Why have people become so rude today? Is this a recent phenomenon?

The reasons why rudeness has become so prevalent today are many. The fast-paced and high-stress nature of modern life can take a toll on individuals' mental well-being, leading to shorter tempers and a reduced capacity for patience and empathy. When stressed, people are more likely to lash out at others. Impatient drivers get annoyed easily and honk if you are in their way—it happens often these days.

Impatient driver

Another reason is increased social isolation. People are spending more time online and less time interacting with others in person. This can lead to a lack of empathy and understanding, which can make people more likely to be rude.

The decline in civility today is evident in the way people talk to each other in politics, the media, and even in everyday life. The way we communicate has changed dramatically in recent years. We are now more likely to communicate through text, email, and social media making it easier for us to be rude because we don't see the other person's reaction to our words. The resulting anonymity and distance lead to a lack of accountability and an increase in rudeness.

Certainly, polarization and divisiveness have resulted in people having little regard for others. This polarization often leads to heightened tensions and a breakdown of civil discourse, with people becoming less willing to listen to and understand opposing viewpoints. Speakers' volume of speech often overwhelms the quality of their thoughts creating a disdain for others' views. I'm right and your ideas are stupid.

Lastly, I think the media, both traditional and online, play a role in shaping societal norms and behavior. The rise of sensationalism, reality TV, and aggressive talk shows can contribute to the normalization of rudeness and incivility.

What can we do to address the problem of rudeness? One thing we can do is to teach our children and grandchildren the importance of being polite and respectful to others. This should start at a young age and continue through their formative years.

We can model good behavior ourselves. If we want others to be civil, we need to be civil ourselves. This means being polite, respectful, and considerate of others. We should try to put ourselves in other people's shoes and see things from their perspective. We need to be more forgiving. Everyone makes mistakes, and we should be willing to forgive others when they are rude to us. But that doesn't mean we shouldn't call out rude behavior when we see it. We should speak up, not in a confrontational way, but in as kind a way as possible to let the rude person know that their behavior is unacceptable. In this way, perhaps, a culture of civility can be created where civility is valued and encouraged. This means being respectful of others, even when we disagree with them.

Thinking about the issue as I was driving along Rockville Pike, I pulled up to a line of traffic at a red light and stopped a car-length away from the vehicle in front of me. A car to my right, in the driveway exit of a store, edged forward to enter the traffic line. Maxine said, "Bob, let that car in." "Sure," I said as

I waved to the driver to come on in. When the light changed, I paused, and the car entered the lane smoothly. The woman driver gave a wave of thanks. I waved back and silently congratulated myself for having behaved politely. A feel-good moment if there ever was one.

10. Pandemic

The COVID-19 pandemic originated in Wuhan, China, in late 2019. It's had a profound impact on the world, both in terms of public health and the worldwide economy. The virus caused millions of deaths and billions of dollars in economic damage. It ruined many businesses and disrupted education and social interactions. The specific details surrounding its exact origin and initial spread are still a matter of ongoing investigation and scientific research. Unfortunately, the unknown origin increased political divisiveness in the United States, created worldwide intrigue, and generated conspiracy theories, many of them extreme and outlandish.

What actually happened? In December 2019, several cases of pneumonia of unknown origin were reported in Wuhan, the capital city of Hubei province in China. The earliest known cases can be traced back to November 17, 2019. Chinese health authorities, working closely with the World Health Organization (WHO), launched an investigation to identify the cause of the outbreak. On January 7, 2020, Chinese scientists isolated a novel coronavirus from patient samples. Initially, it was believed that the virus was primarily transmitted from animals to humans at a seafood market in Wuhan, where live animals were sold. It was soon discovered that human-to-human transmission was occurring, contributing to the rapid spread of the virus.

Despite efforts to contain the virus within China, it spread rapidly around the world facilitated by the global nature of travel and the highly contagious nature of the virus. On March 11, 2020, the WHO declared COVID-19 a global pandemic, recognizing its significant impact and widespread transmission across multiple countries.

My reaction to the news was to diligently track the pandemic and record a contemporary timeline from Jan. 1, 2020, to Dec. 31, 2021. I wrote a 'report,' a spiral-bound manuscript in four volumes, the abridged version of which follows.

It's hard to remember when I first became aware of the novel coronavirus, SARS-CoV-2. It certainly wasn't New Year's Eve, Dec. 31st, 2019, when Maxine and I were guests at Michele and Ray Johnston's home, along with two other couples, for lobster dinner and champagne. There was no discussion of viruses in general, let alone SARS-CoV-2. I don't even recall reading or hearing about the coronavirus infection over the next week, evidently missing the Jan 7th page 13 report in the *New York Times* (NYT) about an unusual outbreak of pneumonia cases in Wuhan, China. Even if I had read it—Wuhan? A city of 11 million people, its population greater than New York City? I never heard of Wuhan.

I also missed the CDC's public alert about COVID-19 on Jan 8th and CBS's report the next night about a new infectious disease in China. Although I don't often watch the TV evening news, I keep up with the *Washington Pos*t and *New York Times* each morning and consider myself current about news events in general, but this one slipped right by me as it did, I think, for many other Americans. The awareness of the coronavirus crept up on me like Sandburg's fog, "on little cat feet."

As January progressed, more reports appeared in the media about how the Trump administration was fumbling around trying to make sense of this novel virus and what its implications would be for our country. Despite my antipathy toward Donald Trump as president, I listened as he spoke on Jan 22nd on CNBC that he was "not worried," "we have it totally under control," "it's just one person coming in from China," and "it's going to be just fine." After being in office for three and a half years, Trump's daily misstatements, exaggerations, and outright lies made me skeptical of what he was saying. My mistrust was confirmed when HHS Secretary Alex Azar declared a public health emergency a short while later prompting Trump to issue restrictions on entry into the U.S. of non-U.S. residents coming from China. Strangely, U.S. residents were exempted as well as people coming from Europe. I didn't understand why *anyone* returning from China would be exempted since the virus didn't discriminate between U.S. residents and non-residents. The number of U.S. cases reported on that day, Jan. 31st, was seven. No deaths had yet been reported in the country.

Notwithstanding the travel restrictions that began on Feb 2nd, the number of cases in the country stood at eleven with no deaths, people were entering the U.S. in large numbers. At the time, it wasn't known that asymptomatic carriers of the virus posed a risk for contagion to others. Ultimately, the U.S. totaled 103,436,829 cases of Covid-19 with 1,127,152 deaths (as of July 2023). No other country had more cases or deaths.

I became obsessed with recording the pandemic news. I learned that Johns Hopkins University created a coronavirus website documenting COVID-19 cases in the U.S. (all 50 states, the District of Columbia, and Puerto Rico) and worldwide, including deaths from the disease. The data were updated almost hourly. I kept a spreadsheet of the cases and deaths in the U.S., MD, VA, and D.C., updating it daily. I re-subscribed to the *New England Journal of Medicine* and began to read weekly articles about the coronavirus and COVID-19. I also subscribed to *The Atlantic* as well as *The New Yorker* reading everything on the pandemic and Trump's ineffectual efforts in responding to it.

White flags commemorating U.S. COVID-19 deaths

Given my interest in photography, I took photos of what life was like during the pandemic. Venturing outside, masked and gloved, I captured images of people wearing masks, waiting in lines at the grocery store, at an ATM, picking up take-out meals at restaurants, and socially distancing while walking or riding bicycles. My attention was drawn to signs in store windows, on sidewalks, and in grocery stores directing people where to stand. There were few cars on the roads, almost no traffic, and only a few people exercising. Some wore masks, others didn't. The CDC said initially wearing masks outdoors wasn't necessary, but as hundreds and thousands of cases mounted, the CDC reversed itself and advised everyone to wear masks when they were out in public.

Some of my photographs later wound up being published in the Nov/Dec 2020 issue of *Bethesda Magazine*.

Life during the pandemic

As I recorded the timing of events about what our political leaders were saying and doing, I noted confusion and mixed messaging. It became clear we couldn't rely on Trump or his Administration to initiate an aggressive, coordinated response to counter the pandemic, but what about the governors and local politicians? Could they marshal resources to give us guidance on what we could do to protect ourselves? Sadly, although they did a much better job than the federal government, the states were ill-equipped to provide enough masks, gloves, swabs, personal protective equipment, and COVID-19 test kits. The states' appeals to the federal government for help went unanswered. Trump's approach was to leave the problem of the pandemic to the individual states, saying repeatedly, that we were "rounding the corner," despite the number of new cases in the U.S. continuing to rise into the millions, and deaths into the hundreds of thousands.

On March 30th, Gov. Larry Hogan (R-MD) issued a stay-at-home order here in Maryland virtually shutting down the entire state. Schools, theaters, libraries, and museums were all closed. Everything stopped. That is what a pandemic does—it shuts down pretty much all human interaction, except for hospitals, healthcare workers, and emergency personnel—police, firefighters, and rescue squad first responders. All nonessential businesses were ordered closed. Essential businesses could remain open—groceries, pharmacies, and amazingly, gun stores. As Tom Freidman wrote in an *NYT* op-ed piece, life changed from BC to AC (before coronavirus to after coronavirus). What about us? How did we adapt? What was pandemic life like?

At first, Maxine and I were diligent in following the C.D.C.'s guidelines—venturing outside only when necessary, wearing masks, and gloves, and using hand sanitizer. Upon our return home after venturing out, we used nasal rinses and washed our hands often. We made fewer trips to the grocery store, and did not go to any restaurants, theaters, museums, or movies ... they were closed anyway. We went outdoors, weather permitting, for brief periods of exercise, wearing masks and observing social distancing as was recommended. As the pandemic continued, we eased up in our precautions to some extent, not using the nasal rinses as frequently, going to the grocery more often, eating occasionally outdoors, or bringing in take-out, and playing pickleball, outdoors only, with a select group of people several times a week. I later learned that the name for limiting one's contacts to the same group of people was called being in a 'pod,' or 'bubble.' Some of us wore masks while playing pickleball, others did not, and we avoided close distances.

Since we had glorious Fall weather, we were able to meet our building friends on the roof for wine and snacks in the late afternoon several times a week. We were all masked and kept our 6 ft.+ distance separation. Everyone looked forward to socializing given the pandemic circumstances. On occasion, we got together with Lauren and the kids, either in their house or our condo, but we wore masks and socially distanced. Later we relaxed and didn't wear the masks inside the house or apartment.

A lot transpired since President Biden took office in January 2021. Vaccination rates increased, especially in blue states, death rates fell, but not to zero, and people acquired natural immunity from having the active infection. In September 2023, the CDC approved a new Covid vaccine. Whether we will ever be free from this virus is a question no one can answer. It's been three years since the Covid era began and the genome of the virus has changed several times, making it more contagious, but, fortunately, not more lethal. People are still becoming infected, despite immunizations and prior infections. I agree with many Infectious Disease experts that COVID-19 will become endemic and that, like influenza, we will need to be vaccinated every year to be protected against new Covid strains. Unfortunately, some people don't feel as we do .. they deny the realities of the pandemic and the seriousness of the infection. They refuse to be vaccinated. They promulgate conspiracy theories and support hard-right politicians who promote denialism to the detriment of everyone. What a scourge this virus has become.

11. Violence

Each day, at least one teenager, especially black teenagers, is shot to death in Washington, D.C. Some are intentional killings; many others are random events, like kids walking home from school, or being accosted while running an errand. These shootings are individual, not mass shootings defined as the shooting or killing of four or more people. As I write this in the first week of September 2023, there have been a staggering total of 484 mass shootings in the U.S. this year amounting to almost two incidents per day, according to the Gun Violence Archive. This is not an unusual year—there were 645 mass shootings last year, and 690 in 2021.

While vacationing in Australia for three weeks last month and talking with people in Melbourne and Sydney, we learned that there have been virtually no mass shootings there since 1996. At that time, a lone gunman killed 35 people at a café in Port Arthur, Tasmania, with a military-style weapon. Almost immediately afterward, the prime minister and parliament passed a gun control law limiting the licensing and ownership of guns and banning all semi-automatic rifles. A gun amnesty program resulted in the surrender of thousands of unlicensed firearms. Since then, there have been only three mass shootings in Australia, in 2014, 2018, and 2022, primarily acts of domestic violence.

What's happening? Why is the United States different from virtually every other developed country in the world?

One reason often given is the widespread availability and accessibility of firearms in the United States. I fully agree. The Second Amendment of the U.S. Constitution protects the right to bear arms, and the country has a long-standing tradition of gun ownership. However, the ease of obtaining firearms, including semi-automatic and assault-style weapons, without stringent background checks and waiting periods, has led to misuse and violence.

According to the *New York Times* Science section (6/27/23), in 2020, 22 million guns were sold, 64% more than in 2019. More than 8 million of them went to novices who had never owned a firearm, according to the NRA, the firearm industry's trade association. Homicides from firearms increased that year to 19,350 from 14,392 in 2019. The number of lives lost to guns rose again in 2021, to 48,830. That's almost 5,900 more deaths than lives lost in automobile accidents (42,939) during the same period.

After quashing research into gun violence for 25 years, Congress began funneling millions of dollars to federal agencies in 2021 to gather gun data.

Millions of Americans who had never owned a gun purchased a firearm from Jan. 2019 through April 2020. Of the 7.5 million people who bought their first firearm during that period, 5.4 million had until then lived in homes without guns, according to Harvard and Northeastern Univ. researchers. Unlike historically typical gun purchasers, white males, the new buyers were different—half were women, and nearly half were people of color.

Self-defense is the top reason Americans purchase handguns. Those who were first or second-time gun buyers in the early days of the pandemic were more likely to see the world as dangerous and threatening than individuals who were not planning to purchase a firearm. Buyers expressed fear of future uncertainty.

Those who said they were planning to purchase a gun were more likely to harbor suicidal thoughts. More than half of all gun deaths in the U.S. are suicides.

Experts agree that easy access to firearms does not make the home safer. Instead, gun ownership raises the likelihood of both suicide and homicide. A 1993 paper in the NEJM found that keeping a gun in the home brought a 2.7-fold increase in the risk of homicide, with almost all the shootings carried out by family members or intimate friends. The findings have since been confirmed in many later studies.

Researchers are focused now on the idea that an armed individual is more likely to perceive others as being armed, and to respond as though he or she were threatened, a concept called gun embodiment. The idea behind gun embodiment is that your ability to act in the environment changes how you see the environment, sort of "when you have a hammer, everything looks like a nail." Holding a gun distorts how one sees the world. Stereotypes and emotions influence an observer's ability to correctly identify a gun, and whether a particular individual is armed. One study found that participants were more likely to mistakenly think that a Black person was holding a gun than to mistakenly think that a white person was armed.

Other reasons the U.S. is an outlier among other nations in gun violence are social and economic inequalities, including poverty, unemployment, and limited access to education and healthcare, which can create an environment that fosters crime and violence. Communities grappling with these challenges often experience higher rates of gun violence.

Mental health issues are often cited by gun advocates claiming that people, not guns, kill other people. Certainly, individuals with untreated mental health conditions can be at a higher risk of engaging in violent behavior. However, the

United States is not unique among developed countries in which people have mental health problems. I don't know if access to mental healthcare facilities is more of a problem in the U.S. than in other countries, but if so, that would further exacerbate this issue.

Cultural factors also play a role in that the glorification of violence in media, including movies, video games, and music, has raised concerns about desensitization to violence, particularly among young people. This cultural influence, coupled with a lack of comprehensive gun safety education, may contribute to the normalization of gun violence.

What can be done to curb the gun death epidemic in the U.S.? Gun control laws must be strengthened with stricter regulations and background checks for firearm purchases, particularly for high-capacity and assault-style weapons. Registration of firearms can help prevent guns from falling into the wrong hands. Law enforcement must crack down on illegal gun trafficking and legislatures must close loopholes in existing laws that allow unqualified individuals to possess guns.

Access to mental health resources must be facilitated and mental health education must be improved so that individuals at risk of violence can be identified and treated before they resort to violence.

Many experts agree that initiatives aimed at reducing poverty, improving education, creating job opportunities, and enhancing community development can contribute to reducing crime and gun violence.

I fear for my grandchildren who live in the District. Each day, I pray they will not become a gun violence statistic.

12. It's Hot

We played pickleball this morning at nine am. I was sweating just walking from my car to the court despite wearing a very light, breathable T-shirt and shorts. If I wore anything less, I would have been arrested.

It was hot .... 79°F with 50% humidity. Nothing like Phoenix, the U.S.'s fifth-largest city, which, less than two weeks after the Earth recorded what scientists said were its hottest days in modern history, broke a 49-year-old record with the city's 19th consecutive day of temperatures 110°F or higher. El Paso, TX, has endured 33 consecutive days at or above 100°F; Reno, NV., hit 108°F, while its neighbor, Las Vegas, reached 116°F, one degree shy of its record high. Estimates vary, but perhaps as many as 100 million people in the U.S. are sweltering as part of a punishing heat wave that spanned much of the Northern Hemisphere.

After thirty minutes of play, we quit playing and gave thought to going for a swim. But where? Even the ocean was hot: the water temperature off the southern tip of Florida, as measured by NOAA one day a couple of weeks ago, was 89°F, only to be exceeded by 92.5°F the next week. And this week, the ocean temperature reached 100°F .... bathtub temperature!

In 2023, the planet experienced its hottest June since records began in 1850, and July was even worse. The year ended up displacing 2016 as the hottest year in recorded history. Alarmingly, the eight warmest years on the books are the past eight.

I returned to the comfort of my air-conditioned condo and tried to learn why the Earth was beginning to resemble Venus, the second planet from the sun. I'm exaggerating ... Venus' surface temperature is 867°F ... but the Earth has become unquestionably hotter. Why?

I learned that the record-breaking temperatures are being driven by the return of El Niño, a cyclical weather pattern, and particularly by emissions of heat-trapping gases, mainly caused by the burning of fossil fuels. The latter cause is recognized by most environmental scientists and meteorologists but is denied by some politicians who continue to promote the use of fossil fuels: oil, gas, and coal.

It's become clear to most people that the climate has changed dramatically toward extreme weather conditions: suffocating heat everywhere, severe storms and flooding in many places worldwide, and drought and fires in other areas on the planet.

On one of our RV trips, we found ourselves in Southern Utah on our way to Arizona and noted the drought-ravaged landscape. Hills, once covered with dense strands of pines and aspens, were now covered with blackened vertical trunks bearing no resemblance to their former lives as trees. Roads, adjacent to free-flowing rivers and streams, were now bordered by dry, rocky riverbeds. Many lakes and reservoirs are drying up, and in Arizona, Lake Mead and Lake Powell are slowly disappearing.

During one severe wildfire spell, we could see no sky, only a thick, brown, smoky canopy so dense that even sunlight found it difficult to penetrate. At one campground in California, we saw flames on hills five miles away forcing us to change our plans to visit Yosemite NP. The Highway Patrol had closed the access road to the park, except for firetrucks and fire-fighting crews.

Wahweap Marina, Lake Powell, Arizona

In Europe last summer, the heat caused more than 61,000 deaths, an eye-popping figure remarkable for approaching the 70,000 dead in the 2003 European heat wave, long considered a worst-case benchmark. In the aftermath, it was said that those heat deaths had changed Europe, which would never again be quite so blindsided by extreme temperatures. But the 61,000 deaths last year didn't seem to raise much concern. As time passes, the extremes of heat this past year will become normalized and fade into peoples' memories as just another hot year. We won't know the mortality impacts for some time, at which point the extremes of last year will have passed into the rearview mirror. Making matters dire, global warming is accelerating, with temperatures not just rising but rising faster than ever. Every day, as it gets hotter, we get better at normalizing extreme weather.

The impact of global warming may have reached the tipping point with sea levels projected to rise by two to three feet over the next 75 years. The resulting coastal flooding and erosion will deluge coastal cities around the world. Close friends lost their home from Hurricane Ian that hit Naples, FL in Sept. 2022. Unable to rebuild on the same site, they moved to a new home on slightly higher ground, but even this may not save them from losing their home again.

Alarmingly, it was recently reported (*New York Times,* 6/29/2023) that the Earth's spin has gone off kilter due, some scientists think, to the accelerated change in melting of the polar ice sheets and mountain glaciers resulting in a shift of the Earth's mass. A recent finding has added to the axis tilt: huge amounts of water are being pumped out of the ground for irrigation for crops and homes. When water is pumped out and not replenished, the land can sink, damaging homes and infrastructure. The space previously occupied by underground aquifers is not replaced and hence the Earth's mass distribution changes. The Earth's axis hasn't wandered enough to affect the seasons yet, but variations in the planet's spin greatly affect satellite-based navigation systems that guide planes, missiles, and GPS maps.

All in all, climate change due to global warming not only makes us miserable now but is bringing about damaging and irreversible changes to the planet that, in the future, will affect our grandchildren and great-grandchildren. I am outraged by the feeble attempts that our country's leadership is taking to counter climate change. Political polarization and climate denialism are preventing necessary action to counter the global warming that is taking place now and this must change before it's too late.

We are leaving future generations a terrible legacy—their weather with never be what normal was when I was growing up in the 1940s and 1950s. Our generation, us, we, are doing this to them, and we should be ashamed.

Remember this?

Westchester Drive, Silver Spring, MD – 2010

13. Choices

It was September 1963, and, having been accepted to the University of Michigan Medical School, I was eager to be starting classes. I had rented an apartment not far from the basic science buildings and the hospital. As exciting as this new chapter was in my life, it was anxiety-provoking. I was alone and knew no one in Ann Arbor. I became determined to find my place and charted a path forward for the next four years. I met some classmates and hung out with them. Thinking of what Yogi Berra was reported to have once said, "When you come to a fork in the road, take it."

Following the first semester, I left the apartment and rented a room in one of the medical fraternities. Meeting still more classmates and working side-by-side with them in anatomy and physiology labs, I was gradually easing into the life of a medical student. The next year, I shared an apartment with several classmates and, through them, met still more people, including a blind date with Maxine that a classmate had arranged. Maxine and I dated for a year and a half, got engaged, and later married. Thereafter, any choices of what to do, where to go, where to live, when to start a family, Maxine and I made together.

When I think about the choices I made, I'm amazed at the serendipity of it all. What if I hadn't chosen to go to Medical School after my third year of college? What if I wasn't accepted to the University of Michigan Medical School? What if I hadn't followed up on the blind date recommendation and missed meeting Maxine? What if Maxine and I didn't hit it off? What if we hadn't decided to settle in Connecticut? Although we wouldn't have met the people who eventually became close friends, we would've met other people who would have become different close friends—choices both open and close doors to various opportunities and achievements. What we've done and experienced by our choices has now become part of our past. We'll never know what we missed by not taking the 'other' fork. That road, wrote Robert Frost, in *The Road Not Taken,* the one less traveled, might have made all the difference. But would it have? I'll never know because the road that I took, that Maxine and I took together, has been a wonderful journey with many more ups than downs.

Seven years ago, Maxine and I decided to move to Bethesda after living in Connecticut for over 40 years. Our decision was influenced by wanting to be near Lauren, Amir, and Mia. It was one of the best choices we ever made. It did mean leaving close friends behind in Connecticut, and although we're not near them anymore, we speak with them often, thanks to Zoom and cell phones. Fortunately, we've made new friends here in Bethesda and have enjoyed sharing our lives with them.

While I don't qualify as an expert, I think I can offer some advice for making good choices. Be aware of what values and goals are important to you. Your choices should align with them. Consider the short-term and long-term consequences of your choices. Will your choices help to achieve your long-term goals? Seek advice from people you trust because they may offer you valuable insights. Don't be afraid to make mistakes. Eleanor Roosevelt once said, "Learn from the mistakes of others. You won't live long enough to make them all yourself." Lastly, trust your gut: sometimes the best way to make a good choice is to go with your gut instinct.

As I was ending my Army deployment in Europe in the early 1970s, I elected to end my Army service, return to the

U.S., and begin civilian life. I did not have a job, wasn't sure if I should open my own practice, work for someone else, or go into an academic program. Maxine and I, and the kids, who were five and three years old at the time, came back to the U.S. and spent a month or so with my parents in Connecticut while I followed some leads about possible towns in which to open a practice. One lead in the Vernon/Manchester area around Hartford seemed promising but it meant starting on my own. Unsure about solo practice, I had arranged job interviews with dermatology practices in Tucson, AZ, Denver, CO, and Portland, OR. Instead of flying to the interviews by myself, I dragged Maxine and the kids along on a long cross-country car trip to visit those places. We stopped in Memphis for a week to visit Maxine's parents and then drove out west. We got as far as Denver, where we decided that the opportunity in Connecticut seemed best. We turned around and drove back to Connecticut. I opened my own office and did well. In retrospect, it would have been easier on all of us had I stayed in the Army one more year, taken a stateside assignment, and used that year to look around for practice opportunities while being paid by the Army. I would have had thirty days of leave, time to search for a job in a more organized and less stressful way. Despite my poor decision, things turned out well in the end. We were happy with our decision to settle in Connecticut and are happy now with our decision to move to Maryland.

When thinking about choices made, one has to be careful not to get stuck on regrets. Regret is the emotion that a past choice was wrong and that if you could do it over, you would choose differently. I think we all, at one time or another, have regretted a past decision, but part of being a mature-thinking adult is to say, "OK, I made a mistake. I'm going to make the best of it. And I won't make that mistake again." Fortunately, things often turn out for the best in the long run. At least, for us they have. I know that we'll be faced with important choices in the future. We'll do what we've done in the past—consider the options, choose one of them, and hope for the best.

14. Memories

I started to think about memory the other day when I couldn't find my cell phone. Not the first time that I forgot where I left it. Perhaps the kitchen, or study—no, maybe it's in the car. It's late tonight—I'll look for it tomorrow.

While trying to fall asleep, in that twilight spell between wakefulness and sleep, I pondered memory: that magical recall of morsels of events past, of slices of current experiences, cataloged in that singular ledger upon which is writ the reruns of our lives, and the resource to which we turn when darkness clouds the mind. How does memory work?

Impulses, electrical or biochemical or a mixture, travel the brain's myriad of spidery-web interconnections to their ultimate consciousness destination, arriving whole, but sometimes distorted, or never getting to the right address at all. I marvel not at how the brain performs this impossible feat in milliseconds, but how it accomplishes it at all.

For example: I thought about my room in the Meriden house where I grew up, a three-bedroom cape, on the corner of Carter Ave. Ext. and Highland Ave. My bedroom was upstairs on the left; my sister Janet's was on the right. There was a half-bath between our opposing rooms. My room, which I shared with my brother Larry, had two single beds, one for me along the right wall, and one for Larry on the left. The beds were covered with matching bright red ribbed bedspreads. In the wall between the beds was a double-hung window with an air conditioner. A maple dresser was positioned along my wall from the foot of the bed to about 4 ft from the wall where you entered the room, leaving room for my desk. It was a modern-style desk with a thin wooden top, sleek tapering legs, and two large drawers on the left. Covering the desktop was a quarter-inch sheet of clear glass under which I would put my favorite cartoons or sayings. The walls of the bedroom were knotty pine. Above the side of the head of my bed, on the wall, was a two-shelf wooden bookshelf which I made in Jr. High School. Situated conveniently on it, were a small lamp, a radio, and several books to read. A favorite was Conan Doyle's *Adventures of Sherlock Holmes*. There was a small closet in the wall opposite the foot of Larry's bed and built-in-the-wall dresser drawers adjoining his bed.

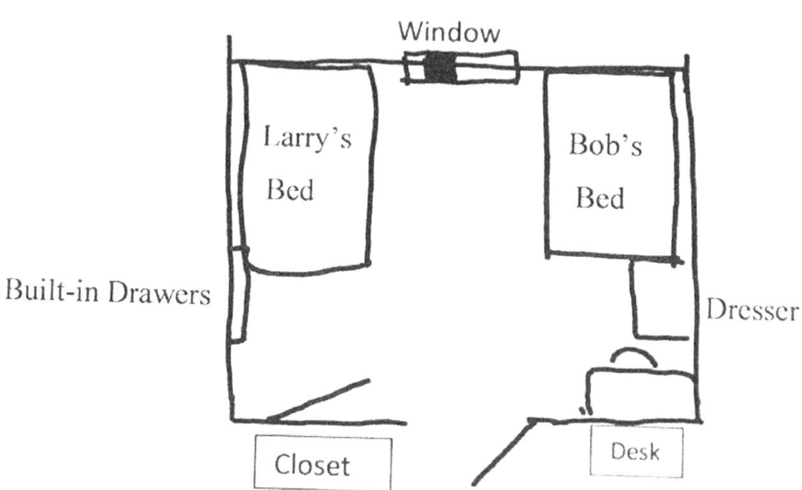

What intrigues me is how I remembered the bedroom in such detail. It's been over 60 years since I last saw the bedroom having left for college and never returning to live there again. How does one's mind work to bring back such a vivid memory?

In medical school, I learned that memories are stored in the brain in a complex network of neurons. When we experience something, our brains create a neural pathway that represents that experience. That neural pathway is strengthened the more often we think about or experience the event. Memories can be fragile, distorted over time, or lost completely by a variety of influences, such as stress, trauma, or simply aging.

There are different types of memories. Memories of specific events are referred to as episodic memories. Examples include one's first day of school, one's wedding, or the birth of a child. A second type, called semantic memory, is those of facts and knowledge. Names of the states' capitals, the periodic table, or the name and plot of a favorite book or movie. Another type, procedural memories, are memories of how to do things: how to ride a bike, tie your shoes, or play a musical instrument.

There is no one 'memory' area in the brain. Several key areas play important roles in memory formation, storage, and retrieval. I will omit the anatomic details but simply note that the brain's structure is complex, an extensive interconnected neural network that computer experts find difficult to duplicate.

Why, at times, can't we recall the name of a person from our past, a place we visited, or stayed, or what delicious dish we had at our favorite restaurant years ago? We may simply forget some memories; others we may repress as a defense mechanism because they are painful or traumatic. New experiences may alter an existing memory causing us to misremember it, confuse it, or forget it entirely. Certainly, emotions play a role in memory distortion and may cloud our judgment making it difficult for us to accurately remember what happened. As we age, our memories become less reliable, due, in part, to actual physical changes in parts of our brain—the hippocampus and prefrontal cortex, sites involved with the formation of memories and retrieval of them, shrink in size with age.

All in all, the phenomenon of memory is surprisingly poorly understood remaining a biological black hole from which the light of knowledge cannot escape.

I've gone on far too long with this rumination on memory, but I'm pleased to report I can remember the wonderful memories about the people in my life—my wife, children, grandchildren, and close friends.

Hannukah, 2008

I'm pretty good at recalling recent places I've been, and experiences I've had. I think my brain is in good working order.

But wait! Where on earth did I put my cell phone?

Where's my phone?

15. That's Funny

Many years ago, Maxine, the kids, and I were nearing the end of a 400-mile car trip. I was driving and Maxine was in the front passenger seat. Our kids, Jeff, age five, and Lauren, age three, were in the back seat, and typical for their ages, they were noisy, cranky, hungry, and bored—the 'aren't-we-there-yet?' kind of boredom. They were wearing on my nerves, and I was becoming testy. We were off the beaten path, to put it mildly; there was no GPS guidance back then. Maxine's map-reading skills were never great, but she was having particular difficulty reading the map as evening darkness fell upon us. Ominous gray clouds ahead weren't reassuring, especially as light rain started to cover the windshield. A few lightning flashes added to the drama. After turning onto a paved secondary road, I turned the radio dial looking for a weather report. Within no more than a couple of miles, the paved road ended. Now on a rocky, rutted dirt road, we were bouncing around like lottery ping-pong balls as I drove along. I was having difficulty hearing the weather report amidst loud static as Lauren upped the volume of her discomfort. I shouted, "Lauren, be quiet! I want to hear the weather." A quiet moment followed. With an exasperated tone, I turned to Maxine, "Have you found out where we are? We should be near the highway." All of a sudden Lauren shouted, "Dad, be quiet! I want to hear the bumps."

We all started laughing so hard that I had to stop the car to gain some measure of composure. We sat there laughing and crying: the tension was broken. Everybody's mood changed. We discovered our way shortly thereafter and to this day, we still find the episode funny. As funny now as it was fifty years ago.

A sense of humor can be a lifesaver as Norman Cousins discovered. Once afflicted with severe ankylosing spondylitis, a degenerative connective tissue disease, Cousins watched humorous movies and TV comedies to bring about laughter that reduced stress and relieved his pain. His recovery, as detailed in his wonderful book *Anatomy of an Illness as Perceived by the Patient*, (New York: Norton, 1979), was no less than miraculous. I began to think about humor and its effects on physical and mental health after I said something that caused Maxine to laugh uncontrollably, similar to the car trip's unrestrained laughter of years ago. Realizing I knew little about the subject, I decided to look into humor hoping to learn what made me think some things were funny and why Maxine thinks I have a good sense of humor.

Little did I know the subject was rather subjective and complex. I always thought that if I found something humorous, it must unquestionably be funny. I felt that there must be some universal gene that we all possessed that made us perceive odd situations, human incongruities, and strange amusements as being funny that would cause us to laugh.

I learned otherwise. Many theories exist to explain the cognitive and psychological processes that go into what makes people laugh at things they perceive to be funny. And not everyone reacts the same way. What one person finds funny; another may not think humorous at all.

Once science begins its exploration of humor, the theories, analyses, and explanations become no laughing matter. Theories abound, each referring to an example of what people find funny. Incongruity theory covers the unexpected, where a sudden surprise upsets expectations and causes laughter. Benign violation theory refers to humor that is perceived as non-threatening or harmless, and which accompanies an inappropriate or taboo violation. Absurdity theory embraces nonsensical situations that introduce whimsy and challenge logical expectations. We are quite familiar with satire, exaggeration, puns, and double entendres that often make fun of others, and mock those over whom one feels superior; all are deemed funny, except to those at whose expense the humor is directed.

Humor is considered to be a form of social play evolving as an adaptive behavior to foster social bonds and group cohesion. Who doesn't want to join a group of people, especially friends, who are laughing and having fun?

A healthy sense of humor along with laughter has been shown in many studies to improve both physical and mental health. Laughter helps reduce stress, improve memory, and unite people by creating more positive communication. "Laughter is the shortest distance between two people," according to the comedian and pianist, Victor Borge.

I'm constantly amazed at how funny grandchildren can be. As youngsters, kids are natural comics; as teens and young adults, they become satirists as they ridicule the pronouncements you've made that they consider absurdities. I've found their snarky blows are better absorbed by laughing with them.

Stand-up comics!

Today, a sense of humor is essential in the battle to maintain one's sanity in this current state of economic distress, climate change, social conflict, corruption, and national political strife. We must address important sociopolitical issues seriously, but I maintain that a strong internal sense of humor and goodwill are the clues by which we can solve the differences between opposing views.

We must learn to laugh at ourselves when we mistakenly do something foolish. We're human, and humans can do stupid things. At other times, we can be remarkably generous, helpful, kind, and caring. Laughter and humor, no matter the situation, are essential in uniting people, adding to everyone's good health and longevity.

Kids at Zootopia.

How can we not smile when seeing someone like Amir enjoying an ice cream cone?

Yummy cone!

16. Seizure

Argghh...the guttural, ictal cry uttered as I thudded to the shower floor alerted Maxine that something was amiss. An electrical storm raging in my brain triggered my extremities' tonic/clonic rigidity and the clenching of my teeth around my tongue. Unknowing and unresponsive, I lay awkwardly on the tile floor awaiting the arrival of help. Thirty-six hours later, I awoke in the hospital knowing nothing of what happened to me or where I was. Such was my first experience with epilepsy, that mystery of neuronal hyperactivity that overwhelms consciousness, transfixes reflexes, and causes loss of sphincter control. Negative results of a brain CT scan, MRI, EEG, and extensive blood work brought reassurance that nothing serious was behind the electrical fusillade. I'm profoundly thankful that nothing was seriously damaged as a consequence of my collapse. Left with uneasiness as to what caused my seizure, I'm bewildered as to the future—will I have a recurrence? Will my being on lifelong anticonvulsant therapy prevent such a happening? I've now added a wonderful Johns Hopkins neurologist, an epilepsy specialist, to the pantheon of physicians looking after me as I enter my ninth decade. My family and many friends are providing wonderful support and comfort for which I'm profoundly grateful.

Adding to the mystery of this medical event is the back pain I'm experiencing. It was most severe immediately after my seizure and I found it difficult to sleep anywhere I tried .. in bed, in a bedroom chair with my legs up on an ottoman, on the couch in our second bedroom, or on the Stressless recliner in the living room, although that is where I'm finding it most comfortable to sleep. The pain seems to be subsiding and I was able to get several hours of sleep in the recliner last night. Encouraged by yesterday's back x-ray showing no vertebral compression fracture, I'm hoping to see even more improvement each day. I just returned from the gym and the exercise has helped.

In the near term, my life will be altered. The state of Maryland prohibits driving a car for 90 days following a seizure. I've already started the countdown, but I am uneasy about whether I will ever have complete confidence that I won't incur a seizure while driving a year from now, or 5 years from now. Will I endanger others in the car with me, or other drivers, or pedestrians? The doctor has reassured me that the longer I go without another seizure, the less likely I will be to have a recurrence. Right now, it's too soon for me to speculate so I am going to put it out of my mind and stay on my medication.

What I've found most helpful has been the outpouring of love and kindness from friends all of whom have wished me a speedy recovery and have offered to help if I need anything. I'm a very lucky guy.

17. My Name Was Bentley

Bentley, 2006

I don't know how I got the name Bentley. I think my human stepsiblings chose it for me. I stood twenty-four inches tall at my withers, had long gray-and-white hair, and at most, weighed 55 pounds at my prime. I grew up in a house with my owners, my parents really, and their kids, my stepsiblings, who looked after me with great love and attention. As a young pup, I had my own crate, but as I matured, I was able to sleep and stay wherever I wanted in the house, but I preferred space under the mud-room counter on a cushioned pad by the front mud-room door.

Officially, I was a Bearded Collie, so named because of my perpetually wet beard that grew down from my chin and lower jaw. I didn't resemble 'Lassie' in any way, looking more like a smaller version of an Old English Sheepdog. My ancestors came from Scotland, and like them, I had herding instincts and was considered a working-dog breed whose job it was to keep a flock of sheep together and protect them when predators approached. I left my parents and litter mates when I was seven weeks old and took up residence with my parents and human stepsiblings in a large home with a wonderful yard and a small, wooded area in the back.

My breed is famously noted for having great enthusiasm and a high energy level, and a bouncy nature because of our peculiar habit of 'bouncing,' levitating with all four feet leaving the ground at the same time, presumably to allow us to look over hedgerows as we guarded the sheep. The move is called 'The Beardie Bounce' and it wasn't something I was taught or learned how to do ... it just came naturally.

I looked forward to my weekly brushing to keep my long hair from matting, but many times my parents couldn't keep up with grooming and just had me 'trimmed,' particularly in the summer, when my coat filled with mats everywhere. And let me tell you ... mats are troublesome and the more you have, the more uncomfortable you are. After my 'haircuts,' there really wasn't much dog left, so my parents said.

Although I lived in a single-family home in a suburb, and not on a farm, I enjoyed running and exercising every day as my dad took me up to the nearby elementary school to play with other dogs before he left for work. The pack of us chased balls thrown by my dad and the other dads who brought their dogs to join the morning exercise club. The dads chatted while we ran our butts off trying to get to the ball first and return it so that it could be thrown again. It was great exercise for me and my doggie friends but not so much for the dads.

Upon returning home, I usually settled in for a nap or just rested until mom took me out when she worked in the yard, or when she wanted company on her walks in the neighborhood.

I was pretty mellow and didn't bark much unless I spotted a squirrel or a dog whom I didn't know. I didn't care much for the squirrels, but I always liked meeting another dog and I learned about them by sniffing their butts. You could find out a lot about someone by doing that, but humans don't do the smell test ... they go online or ask a mutual friend about the person they just met.

On rainy or snowy days when I didn't get outside much, except to do my business, I wasn't very happy. I loved to exercise, to run, and to herd. My parents were hikers and hiking became my favorite activity since there weren't any sheep around that needed herding. My parents got me my own saddle-bag style back-pack where I carried some nibbles, a plastic bottle of water and a foldable cloth water dish. I loved bounding up a forested trail, way ahead and out-of-sight of my parents, then turning around and running back past them circling back to make sure I had them rounded up. At times, they played a game thinking they could outsmart me; my dad would hide behind a tree as my mom continued hiking so that when I circled back and found her, I continued on down the trail looking for my dad and finding him behind a tree, I would herd him back to where my mom was. My herding skills were top notch.

Those were very happy times ... lots of petting, hiking, exercising, and living together. I was able to run and herd energetically until I turned 9, or 63 in human-equivalent years. I first noticed fatigue and weakness and then some bloating of my abdomen and sharp pains in my hind end. I just couldn't find the energy to exercise in the mornings and slept most of the day. My parents became worried and took me to the vet who, after examining me, took some blood for tests and did some x-rays.

While waiting for the test results, my parents learned the old calculation where the seven-to-one ratio of dog years to human years was no longer thought valid. They told me that according to the American Veterinary Medical Association, the new equation was:

- 15 human years equals the first year of a medium-sized dog's life.
- Year two for a dog represents about nine years for a human.
- And after that, each human year would be approximately five years for a dog.

That would make me almost 60 in human years, still too young to be so tired and not my usual energetic self. I thought I might be sick with something.

A few days later, the vet called with the test results. Other than a few words such as 'Sit,' 'Stay,' 'Come,' 'Down,' and 'Go,' I wasn't fluent in human English. I didn't understand as I watched my parents talking on the phone with the vet. They both appeared sad and had tears in their eyes.

When we went to the vet's office the next day, the doctor recommended that my parents take me to Boston to a veterinary oncologist ... I had abdominal cancer; the source wasn't known. The vet gave me some medicine that made me comfortable for a little while. My tiredness was overwhelming.

After a week or so, we went to Boston, an hour-and-a-half drive from our Connecticut home. The clinic in Boston was large and very clean with lots of different smells. I saw several doctors and based on their exams and tests, they set up a treatment program where my parents would drive me to the Boston clinic to receive IV chemotherapy infusions every few weeks. We did that for several months. I didn't mind the infusions, except that I didn't feel well for four or five days after each infusion. It took about three months before I began to feel better. I had more energy, and was now able to go on short hikes, but I didn't have the stamina to run up ahead and circle back as I once did, nor could I run around and chase balls with my dog friends. Fortunately, I didn't lose a lot of my hair.

About nine months after the start of my treatments, I started having difficulty getting up to sit or stand and I was no longer able to control my bladder and bowel. My parents took me to the vet who told them that the end of my life was near. The cancer was too far advanced for surgery. There was the option of returning to Boston for more chemo or putting me to sleep. I was feeling so poorly that I could barely raise my head or lick my parents' hands. My parents petted and hugged me letting me know how much they loved me.

My last memory was of getting a shot and going to sleep.

18. Thanks

Rosh Hashanah, 5784, begins this Friday evening, September 15, 2023, in our secular calendar. It's followed 10 days later by Yom Kippur, a time for personal reflection and repentance, I'm grateful that I'm healthy and able to enjoy my family and friends. For more than several years now, I've moved away from a belief in God, and have tried to focus on being a better person morally and ethically.

I won't be attending religious services at the Temple this year. Instead, I plan to spend my time reading and thinking about ethical behavior and moral values and how to better incorporate them into how I relate to others. Yom Kippur particularly is the time to seek forgiveness for the wrongs that I've done to other people which I hope haven't been too damaging. This approach is one that I do each year. However, there is one 'wrong' that I have not previously, or seriously, considered before. I've been remiss in not expressing my gratitude promptly to others for the kindness and consideration they have shown me throughout the year. This idea has caused me to think about what gratitude and thanks mean.

Gratitude is a powerful emotion that involves acknowledging and appreciating the positive aspects of life. It is the quality of being appreciative, acknowledging and recognizing the good things in life, both big and small, and expressing thanks for them. It should be directed to the people in our lives, particularly family members and close friends, who do or say something kind, helpful, or just unexpectedly nice. This also applies to strangers.

I've read that expressing thanks has numerous benefits for one's well-being. It can improve one's mental and emotional state, increase happiness, reduce stress, and enhance relationships with others. In other words, it's good for your health to be grateful and to express it openly.

For the coming year, I'm aiming to be more grateful for what I have. I plan to take the time to thank people who have made a positive impact on my life. I won't necessarily make a big deal out of it—just a kind word at an appropriate time, a handwritten note, or a small appreciative gift. I must be mindful to be timely with my thanks, express it in person more often, and try to be creative in some way. Most importantly, my thanks must be sincere.

In keeping with this idea, I want to thank Maxine for all that she has done for me over the nearly sixty years that we've been married. While I don't believe in God, I do believe in angels and she is one, for sure. I want to thank my children and grandchildren for all the joy and happiness they've brought into my life. It wouldn't be nearly as interesting without them. As for my friends, many of whom are my pickleball buddies, thanks for your friendship. As the *Peanuts* cartoonist Charles Schulz once said, "A real friend is someone who knows all your faults and likes you anyway."

www.ingramcontent.com/pod-product-compliance
Lightning Source LLC
Chambersburg PA
CBHW040729120726
48010CB00019B/390/J

* 9 7 9 8 2 1 8 4 9 8 0 3 0 *